Sheet Music Notebook

This Journal Belongs To:

____

Index For Songs

Index For Songs

Made in the USA
Middletown, DE
03 April 2023

28176851R00068